# 31 Scraps:

## And A Couple More

Pj Swink

31 Scraps: And A Couple More

Written and edited by Pj Swink

ISBN: 0997189304

ISBN-13: 978-0997189308 (Pj Swink)

# DEDICATION

For Michael, the love of my life, who said I could.

For Wendy, who said I should.

# ACKNOWLEDGMENTS

Thank you, my friends… you know who you are.

When counting my blessings at night, naming each of you…
I always fall asleep before finishing.

That is okay though.
The Lord knows the whole list anyways.

# WHY I WROTE THIS BOOK

Life comes in scraps.

Over a lifetime I have jotted down hopes, dreams, truths and feelings I wanted to remember (or to forget). As fast as Hansel and Gretel's breadcrumbs disappeared from the forest floor, these "scraps" found their way to the trash or were lost in the flurry of living a life.

But as fate would have it, I would find one once in a while. Notes stuck between the pages of an old book or scribbled on the back of a brittle envelope housing a few old photographs. They marked moments like Dropped Pins on the Google Map of my memory.

And then one day a friend read one, and the secret was out.

I have "written" since I could hold a pen, which is not a great feat really. By design, writing is mostly the reason someone learns to hold a pen. Although there is something different about writing and Writing. To say the latter you have to sort of grit your teeth and cringe up your shoulders, as it is not a choice. Some people take great pains to write, while Writing is just painful.

When you Write the words ooze from your soul without your permission.
They haunt you until they break you. And then submitting, you Write.

I have been resistant to call myself a Writer, but at some point the guilt had to be admitted.

Uncloaking deep and not-so-deep thoughts is a scary thing. And although you may apologize for your Art, Art will never apologize for what it does to you.

It is my dirty little secret.

<><><><><>

31 SCRAPS:  And A Couple More

# CONTENTS

# SCRAP ONE

## God Bless the Friends

God Bless the Friends who get me.

God Bless the Friends who don't.

God Bless the Friends who search me out.

God Bless the Friends who won't.


God Bless the Friends who with me agree,

For I find rest upon their shores.

God Bless the Friends who staunchly

Oppose my ideas and my stands,

For I find a way outside of my self inside their doors.


God Bless my Friends,

Bless them every one.

For they love in me something that You Alone provide.

For other than that,

In me there is nothing to love.


God Bless my Friends,

Because I love them.

All so different,

All so valuably rare.

I count myself rich everyday,

Because I found them.

I thank You for their care.


<><><>

# SCRAP TWO

**Your Own Truth**

You learn about life from your parents and relatives.

You learn from your friends.

You learn from schooling and reading and TV.

You learn everything you can from every opportunity around you.

And then finally…

And FINALLY will come eventually…

You just have to go out there and try it for yourself.

And somewhere, sometime you just have to find your own truth.

And if you go out there to find it… you will.

So why are you waiting? Go.

<><><>

.

# SCRAP THREE

## The Redbud and the Oak

One day as a spindly sprout the redbud tree looked at the strong straight oak tree sprout and said, "Why oh why am I so tossed about by the wind?"

And the oak tree standing stoutly up toward the sky said, "Why oh why am I so stiff that my trunk can barely shift in the breeze? I would that I could dance like the supple redbud."

And there was no answer.

One day as a branchy wavy bush the redbud tree wept and screamed as the arborist pruned it and shaped it to his desire.

And the redbud cried, "Why oh why can I not just grow tall and strong like the oak."

And the oak tree towering above straight and tall without pruning said, "What about me? What about me? Do I not need a trimming?"

And there was no answer.

One day the redbud tree fully formed said nothing as it held space at the foot of the great oak and bloomed the most beautiful pink ever seen in the forest.

The grand oak whose shadow protected the pink tree adorning its feet also stood silently, tall and stout as it challenged the wind.

And there was an answer in the silence.

The Redbud and the Oak

<><><>

.

# SCRAP FOUR

## I Just Cannot Help It.

You know…

The words start quietly in my heart,

And press upward into my head,

Are squeezed out to my fingers…

I write.


To not write is to explode an atomic bomb in a tiny glass

bottle,

To contain the uncontainable...

You know,

I give in to the pressure.

I just cannot help it any more.

I write.


So sorry if this,

So sorry if that,

So happy for this,

So happy for that,

You know now that I cannot help it at all…

I write.

And if you write, or paint, or sing, or live a life of art… You

know.

Art presses forth as a new bud in spring,

Exploding from the flower power contained within it.


Art is a giant growing ooze inside of a peeling and splitting tiny

wrapping,

If you write you know my pain.

Let it out. Let it out.


Before it spews.


<><><>

# SCRAP FIVE

## Who Hit The BEGIN PROGRAM Button?

And there it was, already started… stress.
Everyone deals with it and experiences it differently.

Various things stress people… to some one instance may be
very stressful and yet to another the same instance may cause
very little stress.

Funny how that is… probably because it is all based on our
past experiences and outcomes, our belief system, our physical
and emotional temperament, our age, and so many other
factors.

Like tossing a dice with 10 million sides, so many combinations of outcomes.

But out of this complexity a truth dawned on me this morning about stress.
It is sneaky…

Often running in the background of our mind, undermining our energy and efforts passively.
Masking as an effectiveness vampire of sorts.
Like a Windows program unseen until you go looking for it inside the Task Manager.
All the while it works hidden and eats up your RAM.

However, once found and identified…
Windows Task Manager has that little button which allows a person to stop that vampire program from running in the background.
I need one of those buttons.

End Program.

<><><>

# SCRAP SIX

## The Quick Fix

It is understandably and innately human to want a quick fix
and a magic pill...
The ease of altered states, free of pain and discomfort
instantly...
But know it is often a trick and a deceit; so avoid it when there
is any other route.

What became broken over decades is unlikely to be fixed in a
day.

Each Today is the next opportunity to change Tomorrow for
the better,

The true old-fashioned way...

One baby-step at a time.


Celebrate the journey.

Live in the path.

Be, and keep on being in this and every moment.


The goal is only one single dot on the horizon...

Be here,

Be now,

Enjoy the process of getting to there.


The route and backstory gather worth and treasure towards the goal.


Engage in every step.


<><><>

# SCRAP SEVEN

## When I Write

When I write I can barely stand myself.

When I write I am more myself than at any other time.

When I write my thoughts are naked.

When I write I often am afraid of whom I am.

When I write I speak to myself on a page.

When I write I figure out, by writing out, the insides of me.

When I write my darkness is held to the light.

When I write I define and redefine my shadows,

The dark reflections of myself.


And peace is the reward of writing.

And peace is a tremendous reward.

And it is a good thing the reward is tremendous,

For writing is painful,

Like the turning of oneself inside out and pulling the carcass

backwards through a straw.

Good, Pleasant, Bad or Ugly…

The words will find a way to spew onto a page.

The words will not be contained.

Resistance is futile, writing happens.

To burn or not to burn… that then is the question.

At the finished point where the words stare back at me from

the page…

I am done and it is settled.

Time to light the cleansing fire and let it go.

Time to let the warm out of the filled page and allow the

smoke to wisp gently away.

<><><>

# SCRAP EIGHT

**Sometimes I Listen...**

Not to the melody, not to the notes,

But to the silences between the notes of life's tune...

For without the silences there is no song.

Without the quiet pauses... only continuous noise.

As the notes claim the glory, the silences define them.

So much of Life's Journey consists of the long space between

destinations.

Savor the travel,

Enjoy the scenery along the way,

Feast on every moment.

Patiently LIVE right now, today.

<><><>

# SCRAP NINE

## A Friend

Sees you as you are,

And loves you still,

Regardless

In spite of,

And anyways.


Sees you standing in your ideal self,

Celebrates the you that you cannot see,

Knows the you that you are, as you are

And… Before you are.

And recognizes you as you...

Today,

And everyday.


A friend loves you as you were,

As you are,

As you will be.

A friend sees you, and is your friend

Every day.


A friend allows you to see the image of yourself,

In their eyes... a reflection of your own inner self.

Bounces your self view back in a manner you can own.

Returns and yet holds safe the who you are...

Regardless, in spite of, and anyways.


And a friend knows the whole truth of you,

The truth that matters.

How you are as you are,

As You Are...

And the greatest truth...

That you are.


A friend inspires you to reach out hungrily to your greater self,

To walk the bridges you cannot see,

Except in misty dreams and the big scary darkness.


To tread boldly the walkways we all know well,

The known unknown lurking at each next step,

The paths between who you are and who you want to be.

But where each step illuminates under the pressure of your

foot.

If only you press on with a footstep.

A friend reminds you that you can…

If you listen, you can hear them cheering along the way.


<><><>

# SCRAP TEN

**The Path Not Taken,**

The way not trod.

Perhaps it was that left turn, or a right turn,

More certainly it was God.

Who spared me from the ditches,

Who bridged me over rivers,

Who allowed my falls as softly as the snow,

And then salved the wounds so the deep scars would not

show.


A glimpse, a shadow, a forgotten mystery covered in crispy

autumn leaves.

Where is it?

Where has it gone?

Time and fear disappeared together like two giggling girls.

From valley to mountain and all roads in between,

He led me.

He carried me.

He guarded me as I slept on soft moss in the shadow of a rock;

Always with me like the silence between the Tick-Tock of a

clock.


The path not taken, why would I care?

It was not for me or He would have taken me there.

But oh, such landscape where we did go between low and high.

I ponder the possibilities… endless, even infinite and quietly

sigh.

So much missed and so much gathered.

So little gained without multiples of tethers.

Life so excellently full of things, so complex...

And yet often weighted by more than a little despair.


And yet the path is simple.

The way is always true.

Just believe and be willing in the One who owns it all.

Who created it all… that is a Father to you.

Whether stepping or pausing, sleeping or rising,

Doing or abstaining, falling or flying...

Believe and observe His hand at work.

After all we are only and absolutely the tools...

He is the Craftsman...

He is the DO.

<><><>

# SCRAP ELEVEN

## A New Way of Looking

I do tip my head sideways

And look at things upside down…

Sometimes…

And they look different that way.

Hearing a new sound, from an old song.


The louder message is often what is not said.


But hidden in front of us,

In the implied spaces and pauses;

Within the noises of our world and our souls.

The unseen… Right there
Silently screaming in plain sight.

Hear it and know.

<><><>

# SCRAP TWELVE

## Seeing Clearly

"I See You." This is one of my all time favorite quotes. You probably know it comes from the movie "*Avatar*." For me the saying is beyond "I love you." And the movie brings this to the forefront; it is a 'bigger' love and an action love.

Love is an action; I am convinced love physically changes the human heart. It molds and cuts grooves like nothing else can. It fills and completes. It can heal a broken heart. It can chase away the worst fear. I truly believe it really can do all of this.

"I see you" is just a simple sentence of three short words... with even only seven letters, yet it contains so much meaning.

"I SEE YOU."

Ponder for a moment… Do you really ever see people?

Well probably, I have Seen a few people.  People are complicated, which makes Seeing them complicated also. It takes time and attention to SEE someone. Do we really have that much time and attention to spare?

I hope so. Because Seeing is a blessing, just as Being Seen is a blessing.

But seeing is difficult. Many times hurting people stop revealing themselves to others. Oh yes, there is that eggshell layer on the outside, which is the public face. The 'safe to show everyone face' which is safe to show everyone, well mostly.

I think this is why the friends we made as small children remain our close friends even when we are old… even if we have not seen them for decades. They knew us when we were REAL. They actually SAW us and we SAW them.  I think about this sometimes. We spent thirteen years with our school friends, if we knew them from Kindergarten to Senior High. And yet, the friendship feels differently than friendships made as adults. Do you feel what I mean?

Similar happens with people who go to war together. They form bonds that are closer. The rigors and pressures of their time at war with an enemy force them to be Real together.

I think both Being Real and making the effort to See the Real in others is lost sometime during our loss of childhood. It evaporates with our innocent minds. Maybe we find out we don't want to see the Real in people anymore. We find a measure of distrusting. There could be lots of reasons.

Although, hopefully as we age and realize the difference between important and less important things. I have come to believe that being real is important.

It hurts to love and lose. But my choice is to love anyways. It hurts to be real and then attacked or criticized in your real self. But my choice is to be real anyways.

33

None of us know about tomorrow, and we cannot reel back yesterday.

By being Real and by loving people as they are, maybe we will not waste today.

Maybe we will be able to See some people.
Maybe some people will be able to See us.

Maybe we can clearly see.

<><><>

# SCRAP THIRTEEN

### Bringing Our Best To The Game

Winning is swell.

Basking in the glory of success, all opponents vanquished.

Top Dog! So sweet it is to win.

But how many of us ever win at anything?

"Oh, I didn't feel good that day. Oh, the judges were not fair."

"The referees made bad calls. I had to go first... or middle... or last."

There are lots of 'reasons' we do not win.

No, not really.

Not true at all.

These are NOT reasons we do not win, not even one of them.

Please bear with me and ponder this crazy idea I am about to present.

It is a backwards thinking about winning and losing.

Even upside-down and completely turned around… but true thinking,

Maybe.

The only reason anyone does not win (and I mean anyone and everyone) is solely because they do not bring their best to the game.

Okay, I feel the disagreement welling up in your craw.

Let me rub your feathers backwards a tiny bit more.

Even if you place first you are a loser, IF you do not bring your best to the game!

Oh boy! Are you riled up now? What a concept.

Achieve first place and lose! No way!

"My partner or teammate hasn't put in much effort and we are not very good,"
One might say.
This is a perfect setup, just in case one does not place first.
Leaving an 'out,' just in case.
Keeping that self-esteem protected… in mediocrity.

This is only one of many ways to toss in a reason to protect ego and pride against perceived future loss… and thereby guarantee loss.
Not by score… for first place may still be earned… but on a personal level, because one is not fully vested.
So why don't we respect ourselves enough to bring our best to the game?

Fear maybe… oh yeah, that naughty weed.
We fear the baring our hearts and standing naked in the winds of judgment.

What if I do my very best... try my guts out?
Laying everything on the line...

Still placing last. What then?

Oh no, let us setup for the fall and hope it does not happen.

Isn't that the way to preserve self? Hold just a little back in reserve.

Not quite give it all.

Keep an eye on the door.

So tell me can you do that by day and sleep without regret by night?

On the outside it seems to be best to place first, with a safety net.

On the inside, would it not be better to earn last place and have brought your best to the game?

You do whatever your conscious will abide…

As for me in all I do, my goal is to bring my best to the game.

If I am beaten, I will be beaten at my best.

I will bring respect for my opponents, maintaining respect for myself.

It is a persistent struggle to always bring our best to the game.

Against human nature, truly it is.

Backward and upside down thinking.

But if we do not bring our best… we insult ourselves.

We degrade the honor of our opponents, and thus bring
dishonor upon ourselves.

So I challenge us all to be brave and pour out our buckets to
the very last drop.

Bring your best to the game and I will bring mine,

My worthy opponents.

And we will all gain.

And we will all win.

Beat my best with your best and I will strive to do the same to
you.

My competitors are worthy of my best and I am worthy of
theirs.

So let us all bring our best to the game every day of everyday…
and win.

Pj Swink

<><><>

# SCRAP FOURTEEN

**Sadness.**

In an unwise and tired moment I would say to My Self…

Self, I don't ever want to feel like this again.

I want to be sad no more, not ever again.

Please I would beg, not ever again.


And yet, as the unwise moment passes,

And I rest from the weariness of troubles of this life…

When obstacles multiply in number like biting gnats at dusk,

And then grow large like elephants and shake the ground in the

dark unknown.

It is human to be afraid, to be caught and dragged downward,

to despair…

To fall and feel doom.


And My Self would have none of it anymore,

If My Self were the boss.

I know this is a foolish thought.


Not because it is an unreachable goal.

Although it is.


But because human beings need a little and a lot of sadness

from time to time.

This is truth.


For the deep of the deep,

Way down in the valley of our sorrows,

Sets a baseline from which our joy flies upward,

And is measured against the edges of mountains and the sky.


Our sadness marks the platform that only begins the definition

of our ecstasy.


It lends meaning and foundation to our Happy.

It is only from our greatest misery and trial,

That our gladness and thankfulness explode and expand

toward the Sun.

My sadness enhances my joy, when my sadness is over.

It builds the muscles of my soul.


It is with much less foolishness that I say to My Self…

"Do not wish for less sadness, nor regret the walks along the

low paths,

But rather rejoice that from sadness springs joy unencumbered,

And that we can see with unveiled eyes the glory of the Maker

of our souls…

Both in the murkiest ocean depths and in the farthest high

sky."


I know with long-term vision all sadness will end for me some

day.


And in the meantime I live.


I live.

I know there will come a day when I am free to truly sing a song,
More beautiful than can be imagined in this earth-imprisoned mortal flesh.

I am joyous beyond the words these living lips of clay can utter or shout,
When I look up and consider what is to be for me.

Joy unspeakable...
Brilliantly framed against the contrast of sadness my heart has endured, in this long life.
And it may still endure before the beginning beyond death.

Joy,
Born and tempered by sadness.

Joy.

<><><>

# SCRAP FIFTEEN

**Without Regret, I Stand Now.**

Stand with me.

Although the first half of my life would seem
wasted in stupid-ness...
I now see.
Through blindness I have found value in sight beyond that
which I would have had,
If not for those years of blindness.

Life is not about getting, but about giving.

All along I sought with sweat and tears,

What I longed for with every breath.

Driven to acquire and accumulate...

Now I realize was inside me all along.

Not outside. INSIDE.

Not expensive... but priceless.


Like a larvae I wrapped myself tighter and tighter inside a cocoon.

Thinking all the while this was the way to satisfaction.

Yet, in the appropriate season I saw that blossoming forth from that smothering protective cocoon was what truly satisfied.

To just let go.

To be and to bloom.

All along what I needed was not out there...

But in here... inside me all the time... clawing to be free.


Others saw this and told my deaf ears long ago.

I was told that I needed to attend life not for what I could get, but to give what I had...

For my unique perspective fed others in a positive way.

Yet I loathed the insides of me and filed these words away in the folder of nonsense.

I was also told that the artist, writer, or whatever was inside of me was crying to find its way out...
For repressing it would eventually destroy me.
Into the nonsense folder again it went... Along with others.

I now realize they were correct.
I've sought outwardly the things of this world.
Packed them in...
Acquired... gained.
Squeezed and squished them selfishly into the confines of my skin.
Wrapped them layer upon layer into a cocoon.

And festered with rot from within.

The last to know... The pressure did become unbearable.
Yet as I have worked to let go, I now see.
It had to be this way.
For the more blind I was, the happier for sight I am today.

It had to be. In this way. In this order.

NOW a season of change... A radical swift turn.


Time to stop the push, the drive, the requiring, and the
festering pressure...

And just be what was intended for me to be.

Toss aside the wolf skin.

It is okay to be meek like a sheep.

Spit up the raw meat that pleases owls and seek peace.

Stop worrying about remaining steadfastly tethered to earth
and gravity,

Holding greedily to the security of the ground.

But relax my wings and let be what is and what will be.


Fly. Bloom. Give. Be.

Be free of regret with me.


<><><>

# SCRAP SIXTEEN

## The Day I Found Myself Walking

I became Myself.

Walking the lonely road no more, since that blessed day,
When I became Myself.

Not the person everyone said I should be anymore,
I became Myself.

Not living the life everyone thought I should live,
I became Myself.

The easiest thing I have ever done,

I became Myself.

For all along and forever I was just as I am,
Just Myself.

And I had known all along whom My Self was,
I had just lost her somewhere along the way.
And when finally I found Myself Walking,
I knew her straight away.

I only had to have the courage to be her.
And being her was as simple as being Me.

And boiled down to nearly nothing,
The only Myself I have is Me.

Are you You? You can be.
Just be.

<><><>

# SCRAP SEVENTEEN

**Regret**

As years pass and days roll away like so many wild horses over
foothills,
A cloud of dust remaining for a pause...
And then blown or settled away.

I look ahead,
I look behind,
I look now and see...
This moment, in this time.

THIS is where we have to be.

Someday,

If there is a someday for me,

When through the clouds of my eyes you cannot see…

Know I am in there.

Aware, awake…

The body may fail.

But know that I LIVED…

And lived in grand detail.


Know that I saw,

And ran,

And leaped.


Know that I sang,

And laughed,

Wept bitter tears, sudden tears,

And tears of joy.


Know that I feared,

And loved,

Was angry beyond words,

And was sometimes as calm as a sloth.

To be human is to be constantly looking for homeostasis.

Our bodies seek it at all times…

Which means we never hold it,

Or contain it,

Nor gain it except for maybe,

A fleeting second.


And so our minds and our hearts seek constantly for us,

Ourselves at peace.

We yearn for homeostasis BEYOND that of the body,

Yet we,

Are so often ill at ease.


We live on a spinning ball in space,

Moving parts and people all around.

What should we expect except,

A constant state of change?


And so should I this,

Or should I that…

Or will I look back and say this should have been,

Or not have been?

To be human is just as simple and as complicated as that.

Whatever the path or the way the race is run,

One always catches themself... looking back.

What is not so important is 'was it this way or that?'

Choosing to hold no regret is where peace is hidden.

THAT is a fact.

<><><>

# SCRAP EIGHTEEN

## So Fast We Miss It... (Part 1)

30 MPH....that is as fast as anyone should go.

In fact, that is the speed limit in most places here in the Mountains of Western North Carolina. Oh, there are some spots posted at the roaring speed of 35 MPH, but they are more straight... if you drive here you know what "more straight" means.

Where you could pass a farm tractor if you needed to do it, that is straight. But seriously, a lot of tractors go nearly 30 MPH... so why bother.

Here you need to wave, with all 5 fingers...

If you are going too fast to wave, you are just going too fast. I have been in a lot of places where nobody waves. And also have been in a few places where people are stingy with fingers and only wave with the one. But here you wave... all five fingers big, long and friendly. It is just what you do, because people are driving slow enough you can see who they are.

And they can see you too.

You can even stop in the middle of the road and talk if you want. It is okay. Cars drive around. And people talk… that is how we get to know each other. Talking is different than texting or phoning. Although like storytelling and porch sitting, it is becoming a lost art in most places. But really, in a place where the speed limit is 30 MPH you can still do it.

And once you start…
It can be as addictive as heroin or cocaine… And usually won't even land you in jail.

However, even here there are some people who whiz past far exceeding the speed limit. That is why there are black marks on most of the curves. That is why the trees along the abyss on both sides of the road are marked and scarred... and a blessing, because they stopped someone from diving to the green abyss below.

Most of the time bigger vehicles like cars and trucks get caught somewhere and hang up on trees before they take the wild ride all the way to the bottom. Thank God for the trees. They hang in there even when impacted by a soon-to-be crinkled unidentifiable blob of metal and fiberglass. God bless the trees, which take a good hard smack and stand firm holding a vehicle up and off the bottom. They get thumped over and over, and yet live on with a few dents and scratches at varying heights, maybe a little color from the assorted shades of paint. The browns and blacks kind of blend in, but the lighter colors, and even red and blue are noticeable from a fair distance.

Even if cars or trucks do end up going between trees on that rare unfortunate instance... they will stop at the bottom. The other side is straight up. The tow trucks just send down a long cable and pull them back to the roadway. Sometimes in pieces, but mostly they seem to smush together more than fly apart.

But in all seriousness, 30 MPH is as fast as anyone should go...

Years ago we traveled to Montana when by daylight there was no speed limit. I think it was 60 MPH at night. But in the day you could go as fast as you wanted and was able to get your vehicle to travel. At 90 MPH and more I did not see much of Montana on that trip...What I did see is lumped into a blurry memory. I was young then, and going fast seemed to be the thing to do. But in all seriousness, now that I look back...So much is missed when you go over 30 MPH. So much is lost along the way.

And I am getting old enough that I do not want to lose anymore of life's quality to speed. I want to chew my food a bit more and savor the flavor. You know most food really does have a desirable taste when you do not swallow it whole.

Like too many green apples eaten in an afternoon and the total cleanse diarrhea that follows… a lot of undigested, un-pondered thought and emotion get compressed into speedy blurry human bodies on the face of the Earth.

And so there we are, most of our lives... mere blurry human bodies moving too fast to care. And so then we are suddenly somewhere, and we do know by what roads we arrived. Mostly we just have a fuzzy memory of the way.

What about the waterfall tucked ever-so-gently behind that hill on that curve that we missed? It is still there, and as we passed so quickly it called, maybe even waved… And the road noise drowned out its quiet little voice. We did not have time to stop on that day, or any day...

And now the days are gone away.

<><><>

## So Fast We Miss It... (Part 2)

My Grandpa had a tin cup that hung on the well house.
Hanging outside, it was right beside the old smoke house. It
sported a long handle that you would use to reach it back up, if
you were small, and hook it back upon its nail. And I say 'reach
it back', because the little kids had to stand on a fat flat rock
and stretch tall on their tippy toes to do it.

It hung there for all my young life.
Everyone drank from it...
Swished it out afterward and hung it back up for next time.

I never remember anyone spraying it with disinfectant.
Nor remember taking it to a sink to wash.
A swish out was good enough.
Maybe look and see if there was a bug or some little harmless
creature,
Hitching a ride in it or taking a nap.
Fill it up and drink from it.
Oh my, I loved that long-handled tin cup.

Grandpa would say we needed to "Wet our whistle." And I can remember the taste of that water wetting my whistle. How good it was! No, no, no, the word 'good' is not good enough.

How GREAT that water from Grandpa's tin cup tasted! Now nobody passing at 70 MPH stops to wet their whistle anymore. Grandpa is gone and I would reckon and suppose so is the tin cup. I have been too busy to go look or to inquire for the past few decades.

Grandpa's well may even have gone dry for all I know. It is funny how it took forever to become 16, and to be able to drive and do things for myself. So long to be independent, and go out and run about on my own. And the thirty-some years since I was 16 have flown by like a couple of years.

All that driving at 70 MPH…
I am becoming convinced that was what did it.
It was so fast I missed it.

Undigested Life… no time to ponder, no time for moss to grow on a rolling stone.

Do I regret? I say, "No."

I will not do it… for regret is a waste of time.

The time is gone, no need to waste more of it.

For there is even less time to waste as we roll through each

day…

Whatever the speed.


And I have gotten a great deal of great things accomplished in

those years of speeding along at a fast rate. And I am happy

about those things. However, sometimes Life deals you 30

MPH curves. And whether the GPS tells you to or not, it is

time to roll back the speedometer and mosey a bit.


Even if you just mosey for a little while.


Perhaps some people never drank from a tin cup to know the

difference.

But if you ever have,

You know.


There was something priceless and special there. And that

special still exists, now often at some price. But you have to slow down to about 30 MPH to find it. And although I said before, "30 MPH is as fast as anyone should go." I meant on the roads HERE in the mountains.

In a lot of places if you slowed down to this slow speed you would get only the stingy kind of waves. And then you would just plainly get ran over. No 'sorrys' just a 'see ya' and another stingy wave. Maybe a nice someone would honk you a warning, if they saw you in time.

So before you decide to go so slow be sure to exit off onto the curved and narrow roads.
Where going slow is safe and even celebrated…

As the rest of the world flies on by and mostly fails to even notice.

<><><>

# SCRAP NINETEEN

**Tempering in The Valley.**

Have you ever noticed when you make a virtuous statement, or take a stand against evil, there is a "push back"? It is a tempting, a descent into the valley where your stand and words are put to the fire? Always. Watch for it, it is relentless.

Doubtlessly, it is there every time.

And so I have a gentle, calm life when I am on the mountain.

But when I make a stand...
I am felled to the valley, where the winds seek to torment me. A place where as I raise my hands in rejoicing, the heavens and the mountain tops seem so far away. The dead undead of the

darkness seek to eat my flesh and devour my soul. Thankfully, neither my body, nor my spirit, nor my soul belong to me, but are held by the Master who cares wherever I am.

And the terrors of the valley would yield me, urging me back to the comfort of the mountains, if they had their will. But THY will be done. And my will and the wills in the valley do not matter.

"If I ascend up into heaven, thou art there:
if I make my bed in hell, behold, thou art there."
Psalms 139:8

Because, again...
Nothing I have belongs to me…
It never did.

Now I have willingly subjected it all away to the Who that loves me, all is lent to me to use in each moment until I am someday finished. Even until that day when I am used up, and wisp away to the Great Mountain.

Where all of this will be a memory and a story to share...

Threads in His Masterpiece and His Work.

A fragment of His Glory Story...

The part we joy to witness in this flesh.

I long for the day where we will be able to see and touch in person the scars in The Hands and The Feet, the Spearing Scar in The Side, the Thorn-marks on The Head. That moment when our tears will be dried and all our wounds healed. But that day is not yet... He is still making us what we need to be.

My continued praise is to Him who cares enough to make us useful from the miry clay. Vessels in all shapes and sizes, all for specific uses...so none can look at another and judge rightly. We are all being made perfectly as He wants us, to each be for His use.

Again...

Have you ever noticed when you make a virtuous statement or take a stand against evil that there is a "push back"? Ever noticed the tempting, the descent into the valley where your stand and words are put to the fire?

YES, and every word said that is not HIS among them will be burned up and tossed away in ashes, until His Word stands alone in us. He is pulling us into line with Him. Do you see it?

He is heat tempering my words on this day...
And it hurts.
But I am glad that He does it.
That is the only way in the making of a useful vessel of clay.

<><><>

# SCRAP TWENTY

## Boot Tracks in the Snow

Woke up remembering when I was not much over knee high.

When I wore tiny black boots and snow was as deep as my

thigh.

Dressed in many layers, and gloves and knit hat.

Had on so many warm clothes I had to have looked really fat.


But warming by the fire we were not to stay.

Out to the truck and then to grandma's we would go for the

day.

I remember waiting at the doorway as Daddy made first tracks.

That his feet were big was truly a fact.

I took a deep breath of the cold biting air.

Planning and fretting as I watched him, how I might follow him there.

Two of my feet would fit into only one of his tracks.

And I could jump from one track to the other diagonally from left to right and back.


But Daddy said no, just step high and take big steps like him.

And although barely able, I did like he said.

Making it with one booted foot per track I landed into each of them.

Left right left, right left right, and I did it just like he said.


I have found through the years my Daddy was more right and more right.

Those years when he instructed me and protected me both day and night.

And after much life I still remember and still know.

I can do it as long as I put my little boots in His big boot tracks in the snow.


<>< ><>

# SCRAP TWENTY-ONE

## Teenagers

Such a paradox… grown up kids.

Want to do everything on their own.

Have their own glory.

Have their own rewards.

Full of zest and zeal.


Having little or no experience in the REAL WORLD…

Unsoiled and un-jaded, fresh and full of vigor and newness.

Have an ideal of how things are or should be…

But not a reality of such, as in having done things in the big
world.

And this is okay.

Like standing at the threshold big wide world,

With enough 'umph' to go leaping out that door into the
known-but-not-so-known.

Pure fire and no coals.


I think they used to say "all Hat and No Cattle"…

Something like that anyways, in describing "new" cowboys.


I remember being a teenager.

Jumping off into life with energy and drive. Dauntless.


I remember the falls, and the get-ups. More falls and more get-
ups.

Like a toddler learning to walk… just emotional toddling
instead.

Toddling with my head and my heart and my ever-squishy
ever-changing paradoxical feelings.


This morning I was thinking about the revolving stages of life.

Pondering the repeats and redos where the time and context
changes.

How we loop back or forward through the same process,
The same story written differently time after time.
Like concrete curing… a layer at a time for many decades.
That is how we humans are.


We wade through so much stuff during the teenage years,
And somewhere in our twenties or thirties maybe realize our
parents were not so dumb,
As we had thought.
We were also not as brilliant as we had thought.
Life was not as ideal and mountains were not so easy to scale
as we had thought.


We learned to not fall completely to the bottom of the valley
every time we slipped a foot.
We learned that being on the top of the mountain waving your
arms often makes you a target.
We learned that the more we learned the more we needed to
learn.
Because the more we learned, the less we knew.
We began to soothe and settle.

As toddlers it is a physical struggle.

As teenagers it is an emotional struggle.

And maybe somewhere later, in our 40s or 50s it becomes a spiritual struggle.

 It may not roll out like that for all others, but it has followed that path for me.


First I found my Legs,

Then I found my Self,

And finally I have found my God.

And none were as I began to think in the beginning,

But with time and trials I discovered and intimately realized the reality of each.


Funny thing is, all the time none of this was gone from me...

Never was I without legs, never without my self, never did God abandon me and leave me alone.


And yet, I had to walk to find my legs.

I had to go away searching for my self to find she was here all along.

And, I had to try and try and try again, regretting and fretting,

law-abiding and fearing,

Tumbling in turmoil, convicting, and searching...

Just to find He is with me, even in me all the time.


Funny, how life is.


You have to live it to understand how to live it.

And once you live it those days are then already gone away.

Like water through your fingers or sand washing away with the

tide...

There is no feeling it until you have felt it....

There is no holding on to time,

It rolls on as we walk beyond.


<><><>

# SCRAP TWENTY-TWO

## The Difference Between Mom and Grandma...

You know you are a mom when, the formerly disgusting semi-solid multi-colored oozes from your child's various orifices can be wiped with your left hand, a cracker in your right hand, while Face Timing with a friend about the joys of motherhood.

You know you are a grandma when, you move to offer to sponge up the body emissions noted above and are waved off by the cracker-holding hand.

You know you are a mom when, you find one shoe in the minivan and become waist deep in a search of the vehicle, and still find no matching shoe.

You know you are' a grandma when you find 7 shoes, none of them a pair, and you just smile.

You know you are the mom when there are 3 of everything that comes in pairs.

You know you are the grandma when you make a habit of returning 7 unmatched shoes, twice per week.

You know you are a mom when you find yourself saying, "No more tea or ice cream before bedtime."

You know you are a grandma when you are snuggling and sharing tea and ice cream in bed with your grandkids way past everyone's bedtime.

You know you are a mom when you see grandma letting your kids do things she would have NEVER let you do as a child.

You know you are a grandma when you say, "It's okay."

You know you are a mom when "toys all over the floor" is a frustrating issue.

You know you are a grandma when "toys all over the floor" means it has been a great day.

You know you are a mom when your grown son leaves home with a one-way airline ticket to another country, and you just want to paint something.

You know you are a grandma when, you show up with paint.

You know you are a mom when you often look very serious and are always tired.

You know you are a grandma when you smile a lot and take frequent naps.

The difference between mom and grandma is that one works all the time and the other is grandma.

<><><>

# SCRAP TWENTY-THREE

**The Short List of Exciting Things...**

1. Thunder splitting the air in the sky and shaking the ground.

2. Little kid giggles.

3. The intense dive of an eagle onto a streaking rabbit.

4. A look down from the mountain's edge.

5. A look up a cliff face.

6. The ground giving way underfoot.

7. The burbling of a creek.

8. Tree trunks crackling as they sway in the wind.

9. The sting of a bee.

10. A hug from Grandma.

What makes life exciting?

I think my best answer would be CONTRAST. Some would say drama or danger…
I like neither of those.
Drama is tiring over time and danger is just plain scary.

When I was a kid there was an old man who sat in front of us in church who called me a "Stick in the Mud". Okay, guilty as charged. I tend to be a Stick in the Mud.

But I do like exciting things.
The contrast of things...
The edge of things where a change happens.

It is this contrast, this edge of things that tells me I am vibrantly alive.
If you are going to be a stick, be a living stick.

Even being stung by a bee, not pleasant… actually horrible and painful…

But here I am in the flesh, a breathing and feeling human.

And if a sting of a bee could bring my Grandma back to hug me…

I would gladly be stung every day.

Because in contrast to everywhere else in the world, there is no place like Grandma's House.

My best memories are of Grandma's House, remembrances of fort building in the living room out of kitchen chairs and old sheets on rainy days. Lying crossways in Grandpa's recliner eating grapes like a baby bird as Grandma carefully placed each one on my tongue. Listening to Cardinal Baseball on the radio and sipping Ginger Ale.

Biscuits with honey and butter.

Fried Chicken on Sunday afternoon.

Orange Crush Soda Pop and Vanilla Ice cream mixed up in a bowl.

There was never a worry at Grandma's… I saw what she did to that poor Blue Racer snake that chased me out of the yard and onto the porch. She must have heard my shrieks of panic. I was so small and the stone steps so big that I had to put my knee up to climb each one. And I made it to the steps and was climbing as fast as I could when Grandma passed me with garden hoe in hand. I turned around at the top, out of breath, and sat on my safe perch watching her slay the Blue Racer.

It never stood a chance.

Her hoe was flinging dirt and snake pieces up into the air above her head with every backswing. Later she asked my Dad to confirm that the snake was a Blue Racer. He went out into the front yard and looked. He had a funny grin on his face when he returned. Said he didn't know what kind of snake that was. He couldn't tell, being as there was not one single piece big enough… scattered around the hole in the ground she had chopped.

What makes life exciting?

The little things, the priceless things, the good times with the ones you love… the contrast. And we have to see some stuff, and do some stuff, and be without some stuff to realize just how blessed we are today. And how blessed we were, and am…. to be able to still hold tight to the memory of wonderful yesterdays washed on past.

Savor every moment, every breath with those you love.

<><><>

# SCRAP TWENTY-FOUR

**Young Man.**

I am not really a stalker, I just like to stand and watch you
sleep.
I am not really obsessed with you; just think about you all the
time.

I am not on drugs, just cannot help enjoying the smell of your
clothes.
Clean and dirty… on the floor and in the closet.

I do not mess with your things while you are away, just sit
among them breathing deeply with my eyes closed.

It is not creepy when, if your father did not prevent me,

I would eliminate all silly girls from around you.

It is only a harmless fantasy... I do not feed it... much.


It is not weird, although you may find it a little scary...

How much I love you my son.


<><><>

# SCRAP TWENTY-FIVE

## The Path Behind... (Part 1)

Walking in the woods, along creeks, and over rocks was a Sunday afternoon family pastime when I was a kid. My Dad, with all the possible necessary equipment on body, would lead the way. A pistol, hatchet, matches, knife, long-sleeved flannel shirt, maybe a flashlight... There was no cell phone for 911 nor GPS for directions...

And off we would go, prepared for nearly every disaster.

Mary Hollow, Jenny Hollow, or just an old trail meandering around a ridge and over a rocky slope, it did not matter to us kids. Dad just took off in a direction and we followed and explored. We ranged ahead, and then behind, flanked and circled. We found everything… sticks and rocks, salamanders and snakes, tree frogs and butterflies, sink holes, caves and creeks.

We were not like Lewis and Clark…. Dad was. He chose the direction and speed. We merely flowed about like wild electrons around the solid nucleus. And Dad turned us loose to play without responsibility or care.

For a while…

We just practiced in our play how to safely maneuver about… the mostly harmless, little lessons that slight pain and discomfort will teach on their own. We saw what ground was solid, soft or slippery. We discovered how to tell what log to step on, and what log to step over. We found the vines which trip and the briars that stick. We learned how snakes crawl out to sun themselves on a rock, sleeping safely in their amazing camo in plain sight yet nearly completely hidden.

We realized the reason to step wide off of rocks was to avoid being surprised by the sleepy snakes who also lay in the cool shady gaps just under the same rocks on hot days. Of course, we were kids and did more jumping than stepping... but Praise God; no snake ever surprised us by biting us on a heel.

Dad watched us without much rein, as we scavenged about like a couple of Wild Mohicans.

For a while...
And then Dad began to teach us how to take the lead, to be responsible for ourselves, to know how to participate in, even execute, our own rescue should we encounter some measure of disaster.

"You know the road looks different when you turn around to go home. Even following the same path back to where you came from...it looks completely different. That is why people get lost," Dad would say, "they get to as far as they want to go one way and turn around to go back home. And they have never seen that way before." They have BEEN that way, of course, but never SEEN that way. The same trees and rocks and hills look different from the other side.

His advice: as you go along make a habit of walking a short ways and taking a glance back the way you came and make a picture in your mind. Always make a memory of the way BACK home. That way, when you do turn around to go back home you have already seen what it looks like and then all you have to do is just follow the memory stream in your mind.

Sounds simple enough…It is just the remembering to do this simple task that snags us.

And although this was one of the most simple of many lessons... It has served me well for all my life, when I have remembered to do it… And not just in the woods.

Sometimes a person strides off quickly, focused only ahead, and gets "lost" when they turn around to return 'home`. I have done it a time or two, or twenty dozen times... Failed to make a memory of the view of the road behind... And come to a pause because it was like I have never been there. It is unsettling, but not a time to 'go stupid` as Dad would also say. It is a time to pause and think... another of Dad's lessons. Find what is sure.

What is sure?

<><><>

# The Path Behind… (Part 2) What is sure?

-God is Good. Love is Blind. Time marches on and night will follow day as sure as day follows night. Water flows down on a slope and stands still on a flat.

-Fire will race up a hill, but unless propelled by a strong wind will creep downward, if it goes downward at all. Higher is dryer, lower is moist. Fire will only burn while it has something to burn.

-Unlike people, nature does not plot nor have plans… it only does what nature does. Nature has rules it will not break. Don't drink below where you pee, although it will be tastier… but probably not the kind of taste you want.

-The wind will blow where it will, and as sure as you trust it, it will change on you. Clouds often hide the stars, and also the sun… although the sun we can always trust to come up in the east and go down in the west. Although when we get turned around we could swear the sun was in the wrong side of the sky… and inevitably find out later it was and is just where it should be at all times from Alpha to Omega.

-Three markers make a straight line.... walk from one mark (often a rock or a tree) to the next mark... realign marks ahead and behind and choose another mark... walk to it, realign and choose, and so on... and in a straight line you go.

-If you sit still for a few moments, the quiet forest comes alive and loud as it forgets you are there. If you move, it watches you and is silent as it covers the best part of itself from your view.

That concludes the short list of sure things.…. there are more.

Many things are sure in the woods, just as many things are sure in life. One thing for sure is that there will be times of uncertainty.

In times of uncertainty there are always at least some things we do know for sure. And when we are lost it is an opportunity to ponder them as we take a pause. So Self, remember what I learned from my wise Dad. When I am lost, pause and think about the SURE things.

One sure thing is that many times we do end up following a road back just the same way we came. We feel as if we have accomplished nothing, having made a journey to a dead end and then back, a waste of time and energy. But as we take a pause, and gain another perspective it is possible, actually probable, that this feeling telling us we have failed is just not true.

Much like being lost in the woods and FEELING like a path is the way... without pausing and addressing the 'sure things`... actually, even probably, will get you and then keep you lost. Circling and confused, it will not lead safely home again. It is a dangerous time, when you travel back along the way you came. It is a time to not be careless, but alert. It is an opportunity to practice and assess purpose and to be diligent you do not lose yourself or a part of yourself somewhere along the way.

This life is full of highways, paths, trails, and two-tracks.

Sometimes even, we are lead or choose to go off-track, or off-road along cut-throughs or detours or even ditches. Many voices, winds of change, journeys of the heart or mind lead us, guide us or compel us by fear or duty or some other greater or lesser force to travel where we never pictured ourselves in all our imagining.

And so we go... and sometimes come back along the same trails. Sometimes we go as Lewis and Clark, the responsible leaders, alertly on point. Sometimes we meander, even wander along barely in sight of a leader like wild children free in the forest.

So when we go and then find ourselves returning, we should be sure we arrive back with ourselves intact, with our truth fortified. For the paradox of these times is that arriving back with ourselves intact is actually moving forward... even when it seems not. It is not time nor energy wasted, but rather time and energy spent.

The forest altered by our passing, even slightly, is a forest altered by our passing.

The little bits of ourselves left there, not lost there, but left there...will regenerate back to us as a salamander grows a new tail... looking just like the old one, only not.

Our intentions pure and harmless, without causing wanton destruction nor senseless desolation, without treasures discovered nor goals captured... we recant our steps along the same footprints sometimes. And that is okay.

Only a leaf turned or a footprint in the clay seems to be the result of our journey, yet the true results are the greater unseen changes of the heart. Things seem to be the same, and yet are not. Things made better that cannot be seen, until the future chooses to manifest them in the future's own time.

Like the lessons a father teaches to wild and roaming children, who seem to be neither listening nor watching... But who are absorbing all. The road there and back trusting is a road there and back free of regret.

Note to self: Trust what you know. Feel the pain and then let it go. Poke the elephant in the butt who tries to sit on your chest.

He will move, if you inspire him to retreat. Make regret flee with haste, for it is a great waster. Only in the Lord, Our Father, may we find peace and rest.

He is sure.

<><><>

# SCRAP TWENTY-SIX

**Love.**

There are many kinds of love in the world and in people's hearts. In American English we say one word: "Love." And according to merriam-webster.com, this one word may mean nine numbered definitions, plus additional explanations of definitions for kids and new English learners.

I am personally very strict about the word LOVE... when I define it to myself. Basically, if it is necessary to put anything after it in a sentence, it is not the kind I want in my heart. And it is not the kind I prefer to enjoy from someone else's heart.

I love you.

It should end there.

Within myself I try to make it end there.

Anything else is a contract, not a gift.

Love that is not a gift is no longer priceless.

I love you. Is agape (Greek). It is priceless. It has no
conditions, no earning, is not a trade… it requires nothing else.
Just I LOVE YOU. And a period at the end… that is a Gift.
Anything else is a trade… you do or you give something, you
be something, you cease from something. If anything is added
on as a requirement, no matter how small the requirement…
Then it is just a trade, merely a merchandise transaction.

A gift is free. Agape love is free.

I love you… with something added like:

But

In spite of

Because of

When

As much as

As little as

Is not agape.

Agape love can only be gifted to another or one's own self. Once given it no longer nor forever belongs to the giver again. There can be no ties to it to the giver anymore. It belongs to the one who receives it from the giver. When we were kids we said, "No take backs!" There are "No take backs" with agape love. It does not dissolve nor wither over time and distance.

Agape is not the kind that manipulates. Nor is it the kind that makes you sick. It is the kind that blesses both the giver and the receiver.

Is it True Love? Probably. But the words True Love get so much abuse.

It just is, and it is never-ending no matter what or where. It is regardless. Anyways. However. Whenever. Wherever. Whatever. Always. It is Love at peace with itself. It is the love that heals and chases away fear. It is the powerful version of love.

Agape love is never ugly.

Agape love is just love.

Pure Love.

<><><>

# SCRAP TWENTY-SEVEN

**Water**

Water occupies a space and form given to it by its surroundings. It flows downward with gravity's pull. It is forced upward by hydrostatic pressure. It is lifted as vapor by the heat of the sun.

We are much like water. Much of our makeup is, in fact, water.

Going with the flow we can be drawn lower and lower until we pool at the lowest point. We can seep or we can roar and rumble. Flowing as a clear river we can make pleasant noises and happy gurgles, and as a dark stagnant pool we can stand still and grow green-yellow scum.

Purified by Light and Fire, we have tendencies and abide by laws that often cause us to repeat cycles of life in different times and different places. We occupy space, yet we are squishable.

When we are clean, we are as water alone. Pure. Most substances mix with us and we carry them along our way. Oil floats on us, dirt muddies us, and many chemicals disappear into us.

Under pressure we can be both highly useful and highly destructive. A power washer can force dirt from the cracks of a porch. A mighty flood can wash the porch and its house away with no apologies.

Under minimal pressure we may lie around like puddles. And if stirred without direction or purpose ... muddy puddles.

The Great Ocean calls and draws us to Himself. We are a part and portion of the Great Ocean sojourning across the land.

May our days of usefulness upon the land be many, and our river days happy. May only a few days be spent in muddy puddles and scum-covered ponds. May we be lifted up with excessive joy to soar the clouds and sail high over many mountains. May we know what it is to be swept to earth by mighty winds and splash down upon surfaces both hard and soft. May we know the lonely darkness of earth's caverns and the Force, which guides and presses us to the spring on the top of the mountain where the birds sing and the trees touch the high sky. May we feel and have joy in the ebb and flow of Life as He moves us where He wills.

May we eventually find ourselves at rest within the Great Ocean and abide there amongst the other well-journeyed water droplets forevermore.

<><><>

# SCRAP TWENTY-EIGHT

## Will You Know Me?

Will you know me?

When I cross the river's deep.

When I complete my arduous journey,

And Rest's appointment I am freed to keep.


Will you know me?

In my glorified body,

Neither old nor very young.

Will you know me when I am singing?

When I am laughing...

It has been so very long.


Will you know me at the shoreline?

Or will you see me coming across.

Will your eyes see something familiar?

As I am one of those you lost.


Will you hug me and call me daughter?

When you left I was very small.

Will you know me when I look grown?

I am still not very tall.

I will look for you at the river.

I will search for you in the pleasant fog.

I will know you when I see you.

I will know your voice when you talk.


I will miss you until I see you.

I will miss you until we hug.

I will miss you, yet I will know you.

Will you know me?

And tell me you have missed me.

When you left I was so small.


<><><>

# SCRAP TWENTY-NINE

## The Sweeping…(Part 1)

Sometimes when we are finding our place in the world we are like seed being swept around and tossed up into the wind. We are looking for that niche in which we belong. That thing we do just like only we can do it. We are having the husk knocked and blown off and away.

We are becoming who we are.

It is a beautiful thing to see someone who has found Them Self and become himself or herself. Everyday I am happy to wake up and meet myself again. Each day is new… still me though. Funny, I was there all along… and just did not realize it.

An acorn and then a sprout and then a tree… all me, everyday… just not in the way I could recognize or appreciate myself… until one day, I saw. And oh my, I got it!

It is my hope all of us get to that peacefulness… where we are what we are everyday.
And all that will, will.
And some won't maybe ever, but how can anyone tell who will and who won't….
We have to hope and believe.
It makes me happy to see it, to witness it.
To hear of the journeys.
To tell of my own continuing journey.

If only I could have spoken to my child self or teenager self once upon a time and said these things. And yet the ignorant struggle of the child, or the rebellion and 'leave-me-alone-I-know-it-all-and-can-do-it-myself of the teen, were only the first and second legs of the long journey still unfolding.

We may not look like what we think we ought to be.

We might not be able to do what we think we ought to do.

But there is a lot of seed husk to get wore off of us in this lifetime.

Sometimes it even rots and stinks before being shed.

The shuck and husk shield us and nourish us and we tend to let it cling to us and we cling back to it. Security and sameness... But the wind tossing and ground bouncing will wear it away. If we live long enough we (meaning the husk of us) will become old and weary… and if all of our hope is in this life alone…. we are so very miserable. Because we will shed this life, like the husk it is, eventually. And if the all of a person is shuck and husk…. so sad. But inside THIS husk-cover is a living seed linked to Elsewhere.

'Every seed shall bring forth after its own kind'…. so what does the seed of our Father bring forth? Our Father's Children. Our hope is elsewhere, while we are here experiencing a journey. It is a grand journey of great discovery, if we pay attention.

We may see niches and point ourselves in those directions only to be shifted away over and over to somewhere else completely new. But like wheat seed being flung into the air.... It takes time and effort to get us to what and where we need to be.

And yet the paradox, we were and are there all the time.

An acorn contains the whole oak tree.... At no moment is the acorn ever anything else than an oak tree baby hidden in the husk.

Think about it... and then do happy, happy backflips of joy.

<><><>

# The Sweeping... (Part 2)

Two things are happening at the same time in this human journey...

First, we are being located to where we need to be to do whatever it is we need to do as being flung and swept ultimately toward that one perfect niche that we are being designed to fit.

And secondly, we are being de-shucked, husked and designed to be the perfect fit to that niche when we get there.

Two things and a time component... It is the journey of our life. We are as much witnesses as participants in the journey.

The Sweeper Designer is doing the work... we are merely showing up and yielding. What does an acorn do really?... It is. God created it. God gives sun, soil and water. God gives it the life inside to sprout. What does the acorn do?... It just is. It is not even able to ROLL by itself. Gravity makes it fall out of the tree. A squirrel buries it in the ground. Again, cannot even make itself roll...

When this process is taking place at first you do not even realize it. Then you start to be more and more aware of the forming of yourself and the niche that you are approaching.

Tension. We feel the tension of the forces that guide us and mold us and flex us against the guardrails.

We feel Master's Hand which holds us to the fire, just enough…but not too much. Like two lines on a graph merging… a specialty tool being made for a specialty task and shipped to the location of the specialty task to arrive and be in service at that time the specialty tool is called upon for special duty. Wow!

We are heading for ourselves and will arrive at the perfect time. Do you see it?

We feel the pressure as we are honed and placed. But how far away or how long the service… we do not know until it happens. A person feels it coming, if they listen and watch. Many times we think of witnessing as a speaking activity…

Much of witnessing is simply paying attention, recording the journey.

For what can we say except we have seen and heard?

If we are quiet and pay attention we can see just how the Sweeper Designer works. He is Amazing and Marvelous. He is perfect in all His ways... so he will Place and Design and Time us perfectly. And so when the time of witnessing comes that involves the speaking and doing, what could possibly come out?

The LIFE that is in the acorn...it will come out.

It is so wonderful when you Get It! When you see it all un-shucked. The day when the lines merged for me, there I was, and everything was okay.

And so when the sky is full of clouds and fire rages and anger is everywhere...
When the only seas to swim are full of sharks and the land is shifty and unstable...

I still know where I am.

The I AM is still in charge and sweeping and He is our Dad, so
He sweeps loving us... His Seedlings.
Can it get any better than that?

We can trust we will be what we need to be when we get to
where we need to get.
The Sweeper Designer knows what He is doing.
That is the coolest part. The story ends okay.
And although we did not write the story, we benefit from
participation in it.
And the ending is a happy one for us.

My job is to quiet the static in my head that keeps me from
hearing what I am listening for and to keep looking until I see
what is in plain sight in front of my eyes. And THAT is a hard
job, DAILY a hard job.

It is a comfort to know the Sweeper. And the Sweeper is not
the wind. He uses the wind, just as he uses the hard ground in
His working of the grain. He is intentional and purposeful,

NOT random and inconsequential. He is mighty and able. And I am thankful that He made a day when we can finally meet ourselves and see we are okay, because He never messes up making us, and remaking us, re-forming, and re-tooling us.

He does perfect work… and that is comforting.

<><><>

# SCRAP THIRTY

**I can see clearly now the rain is gone.**

These are great song lyrics by Johnny Nash.

> "I can see clearly now the rain is gone.
> I can see all obstacles in my way.
> Gone are the dark clouds that had me down.
> It's gonna be a bright bright sunshiny day."

I had never heard it this way before. Yes, the words are the same old words… But TODAY I get it. The obstacles are still there, because the lyrics say that I can see all of them in my way. Without obstacles we are allowed to remain weak. Obstacles build our muscles overcoming them.

I am imagining a house-grown tomato plant, having grown tall and slender trunk and vines. No wind to slap it from side to side. No rain to beat it downward toward the ground. And when it is transplanted into the garden, I have to stake it up or it will break in two when the wind and rain inevitably come.

And yet the wild seeds that sprout from last year's tomato crop grow strong and stoutly. The volunteers who did not require "planting" to grow up in my garden, have thick trunks and solid limbs. They fight the cold, wind, rain….and the gardener who at first sees them as weeds.

It is not about not having problems; it is about walking on anyways.

There are no people without burdens, just people with different burdens.

<><><>

# SCRAP THIRTY-ONE

## Spring

What a great day to be alive! Oh my, after the rain, thunder and lightning last night, walking in my yard this morning was pure joy. Oh wow... the creation is amazing when it "comes alive" in spring. Everything washed fresh and waking up to the new day. The turbulent sky of night turned to a beautiful mix of clouds and sunshine framed against the new green life below.

The warm air makes my hungry lungs dance.
What a wonderful day the Lord has made...again!
It is a good day to be alive. I am simply blessed to breathe!
So even more thankful to See and Know by whose power it is happening.

Just weeks ago it was so dreary cold and seemingly dead and hopeless. The grass was brown. The trees were naked and still. And look now...everything is waking up ... everything is being quickened by the life hidden inside. We couldn't see it, but the life was there all along through the cold darkness of winter. It was alive, but seemed dead.

I am always so happy when winter ends. That must be why birds sing… if they kept it to themselves they would surely swell up and burst, like a seed breaks from its shell. A seed's dry dead shell finally arrives at a time when it can no longer contain the growing pressure from within. And KaBaaaam!... the shell has to cease hindering and let the sprout out. Some glorious day that will happen to us. The sprouts will come out!

The creation expands from within itself and manifests what was long hidden inside...hidden by the Creator until the season was right.

What a great day to be alive!
Have a magnificent day!

<><><>

# BONUS SCRAP ONE

**A lot of tunes play each day.**

A lot of melodies ring out, to which we can sing and we can dance.

Always, a bunch of noise is OUT THERE in the world.

And yet, each day I choose…

To sing and dance to the tune that rises from the INSIDE OF my own heart.

It is the one melody I know for sure.

So…

Let us each PICK the music we each dance to daily.


We each hear our own special notes, our own unique
combination of tunes.
I can be me and You can be you.
One cannot say what some others should do.


So who can I judge except Myself?
Certainly I cannot judge You.


The smart voice in my head says, "Just listen and watch"
The smart voice in my head says, "Only consider you."
I know,
Just that and that alone is more than I can even do.


Let us celebrate…. as we are living, human, beings.
Mine is the only melody I know for sure.


<><><>

# BONUS SCRAP TWO

**Now**

The day a person stops pointing to accolades on the wall,

The day a person stops being impressed with his or her own
ability,

The day a person stops beating themself up for imperfection
and limitations,

The day a person stops being halted at the sight of others'
standards.

The day a person realizes that a person's very best is as good as
it gets.

That day a person improves.

Yes, it is a paradox.

But that day a person becomes more able.

Their best becomes better.

And better, and better....

When not thinking, "Look at me! I am doing so well"... and falling into the ditch on the right side. When not thinking, "Don't look at me! I am doing so poorly"... and falling off to the left. But by just doing the work, in that moment you do the work, performing the best that you can.

Right then.

Not held up to the light of yesterday.

Not held up to the light of tomorrow.

Right then, now.

The best you or I can do.

Now.

That day a person improves.

So let me encourage you, as I encourage myself... just do the work.

Whatever work you put forth your hand to do… do the work the best you can in THIS moment. Do the best you can in THIS time. Now.

With the tools you have, but not resting upon your laurels. Without the tools you lack, improvising, adapting, resiliently thriving.

Not looking back nor forth, yet pulling from the past and pushing toward the future, hands on task excelling in the NOW.

Because in reality, Now is what you and I have.

And everyone can do the best they can do… Now.

There is peacefulness in having permission to do just that.

No excuses.

Just do the work.

Now.

<><><>

<><><><><>

The End.

# ABOUT THE AUTHOR

Pj Swink lives on the western edge of the Great Smoky Mountains in Maryville, Tennessee. She is a wife, mother, grandmother, and writer.

The eldest of six siblings, she was born and raised in West Plains, Missouri.

She obtained a Marketing Degree from Missouri State University in Springfield in the mid-1980s and worked as Business Manager of THE STANDARD Newspaper during Graduate School. With an M.B.A. she returned to small-town life and began a successful printing business in 1990. After 17 years of printing and publishing for other people, she had yet to publish even one of her numerous writings.

It was not the time to show her art to the world.

Selling the printing business and returning to school in 2007, for the following years she worked as a massage therapist. In time, she continued into massage therapy instruction and research, even developing and trademarking her own massage technique by 2015.

Having survived many adventures with her husband of twenty-some years, having raised two sons, and with a newborn grandbaby for inspiration, she began in late 2015 to finish and publish the many scraps and manuscripts laid back from a lifetime of writing. After ranching, farming, printing, massage, and many other activities left unmentioned here, it is time for her to share her own written work with the public.

And I, along with other of her friends say, "Finally!"

<><><>

You can find more information about Pj Swink at:
https://www.facebook.com/pjswinkwriter/